ARMS WIDE OPEN

An Insight into Open Adoption

By

Jane Waters

authorHOUSE™

1663 LIBERTY DRIVE, SUITE 200
BLOOMINGTON, INDIANA 47403
(800) 839-8640
WWW.AUTHORHOUSE.COM

First published by AuthorHouse 10/04/05

ISBN: 1-4208-7854-9 (sc)

Printed in the United States of America
Bloomington, Indiana

This book is printed on acid-free paper.

TABLE OF CONTENTS

DEDICATION.. vii

PREFACE: ix

INTRODUCTION:.. xi

CHAPTER ONE: THE TYPICAL BIRTH MOTHER PROFILE..1

CHAPTER TWO: HOW OPEN DO YOU WANT TO GO?..9

CHAPTER THREE: OBSTACLES TO A SUCCESSFUL ADOPTION: 13

CHAPTER FOUR: FORGIVENESS 35

CHAPTER FIVE: BOUNDARIES 47

CHAPTER SIX: THE HOSPITAL EXPERIENCE 55

CHAPTER SEVEN: NAME THIS CHILD 61

CHAPTER EIGHT: WHAT ADOPTING PARENTS WANT YOU TO KNOW 65

A FINAL NOTE 77

POINTS TO REMEMBER....................................79

APPENDIX A: BIRTH PLAN FOR PATIENTS PLANNING ADOPTION 81

APPENDIX B: ACKNOWLEDGMENT OF BIRTH FAMILY 87

RESOURCES: 89

DEDICATION

This book is dedicated to all the birth mothers and adopting parents everywhere. I especially thank the ones who have let me be a part of their experiences, pain, and healing.

I want to thank Cheryl Bauman, the director of Crisis Pregnancy Outreach, for inviting me to be involved with CPO, for your editing, support, friendship, and being a Christian role model to the girls and me. I hope our next fifteen years is as endearing as the last fifteen! I wish I had a nickel for every lunch we spent together. I love you! Thank you, also, for all the hundreds of volunteers for CPO, past and present, who give so much of themselves and their time to make this such a successful ministry.

I am very grateful to my husband and best friend, Chris, and my close friend, Heidi, who have also been my editors, and all my closest friends and my church family for being my biggest supporters, encouragers, and cheerleaders. Church of the Holy Cross is, truly, the biggest littlest church in Owasso. I love you!

I want to thank my family, my own, and the one I came from, for believing in and encouraging me. Your support means the world to me. I love you all!

Finally, I want to acknowledge that all the glory goes to God! My life and this book have been divinely orchestrated by Him and I am eternally thankful that He entrusted and allowed me to join Him in His plan.

Please feel free to share your stories with me by emailing them to courage2heal@cox.net and visit my website at www.courage2heal.org .
I'd love to hear from you. Thank you.

Please feel free to visit www.crisispregnancyoutreach. org to learn more about open adoption.

Janey Waters copyright 2005

PREFACE:

One of the best ways in which I can honor the young women with whom I have worked for the past fourteen years, is to write a book about what they have taught me as a therapist. In 1990, Cheryl Bauman, the director of Crisis Pregnancy Outreach, asked me if she could refer some of the teenage pregnant girls from her agency to me, for therapy. I was excited about the prospect of working with both the young women and Cheryl, so I accepted. It has been difficult and rewarding work on both my part and the girls' parts, but it has given me a tremendous amount of experience and knowledge of what these girls go through, when considering parenting or adoption. It is my desire to only honor them, and to share my experiences with the many other young women and their families who are facing the same painful decisions and who are reaching out for information and help. I have really enjoyed our work together. You all have provided me with valuable lessons about life and relationships, and I feel honored to have been a part of your growth. You have been an enormous part of mine.

All names have been changed to protect the pregnant! At times, I'll use a combination of several girls' experiences to help make my point.

INTRODUCTION:

So, you're considering adoption. Great! One of the best things that you can do at this time is to gather information about the different types of adoption. There are two choices: "open" or "closed." Open adoption means that the birth mother knows the adoptive couple and has some form of continuing contact with them. Closed adoption means that the entire process is anonymous, which means that the birth mother and adopting couple do not know each other, have no contact, information, or desire to have any relationship with each other.

This book is only about open adoption. There are two reasons for this. Firstly, it has been my experience that closed adoption causes both parties much more emotional pain; and, therefore, is a less desirable option.

In my practice, I have had the opportunity to treat birth mothers and the children of closed adoption, and have seen the damage that the process does to each. There is too much "guessing" and wrong assumptions on each part that is very painful and highly distracting to and interfering with their lives. Secondly, the bulk of my experience has been with Crisis Pregnancy Outreach, which is an agency that promotes only open adoption. In addition, it provides support services to the girls who choose to parent. In my opinion, it is by far the best situation within which to work.

This book focuses specifically on the time period from the birth mother's pregnancy, birth, finalization of the adoption, to a year or so after the birth. This is the most critical time in the adoption process and, therefore, deserves the focus. If the issues addressed in this book are confronted and resolved, then your chances for a healthy and successful adoption increase exponentially.

It is important to note that this book is from a Christian perspective. The agency with which I have worked is Christian-based. Therefore, most of the birth mothers and certainly the prospective adoptive parents are Christians. I have been a Christian my entire life, as well. It would not make sense for me, nor would it be my desire, to "check God at the door" and leave Him out of this most important process. When God is at the heart of this, not only does it increase the success, but it heals as no other counseling can do.

I have had the opportunity to be an integral part of hundreds of open adoptions, and it is my desire to share this information with those who are considering it. I hope this helps you gain a broader base of information, and widens your perspective. I, also, hope that this process leads you to a deeper relationship with God, and that in so doing, you reflect His light in such a manner that you become a beacon for others.

CHAPTER ONE:
THE TYPICAL BIRTH
MOTHER PROFILE

There is no "typical" profile of a birth mother, but there is a typical "range" of characteristics. They come in all shapes, sizes, and ages, races, and hair color. I've seen some as young as twelve years old and some as old as fifty-three. However, the majority of the girls range from ages fifteen to twenty-five. The pregnancies are, usually, the result of a sexually active relationship of a few months, and whose boyfriends broke up with them once they found out they were pregnant. Almost all of the girls have refused to have an abortion because of their own belief system, a fact which continues to impress me. However, most have been "encouraged" to have an abortion mostly by their friends, boyfriends, or parents. They believe that abortion would be the "easiest" answer. They think that it would be quick, easy, and then it would all be over. Actually, nothing could be further from the truth.

Their Living Situation:

Their living situations vary, from living at home with their families, to having lived on their own for a year or two. Most of the girls who originally lived on their own end up moving back in with their parents for support. Many of the girls are from alcoholic homes and who have, also, developed addictions. Usually, where there is alcoholism, there is, also, abuse or emotional neglect. However, many are from homes where there is no significant level of dysfunction. The families of these girls are normal, law-abiding, Christian citizens, who have appropriate guidelines and expectations from their children.

Some of the birth mothers are without a means of support, so the agency with whom I work, places them with "host families." These families volunteer their homes for the duration of the girls' pregnancies. Then, sometime after birth, the girls either return to their own homes, or have the option of living at the "Transitional Home," which is offered by the agency. They can live there for up to a year, or until they can develop a means by which they can support themselves.

Looking for love in all the wrong places:

Although there is a small percentage of girls who lead a promiscuous lifestyle, the majority of the girls are just looking for love in all the wrong places. The pregnancy is usually from a relationship with their boyfriends in which they were sexually active. The ones who are sexually active with many partners are, usually, just wanting to be loved or to feel special, which may have been absent in their childhood. For most women, young and old, as soon as they have sex with someone, they get emotionally attached, whether or not it's a healthy relationship. I have found that the girls who are desperate to be loved are always with an unhealthy male, which have many characteristics in common with their fathers. They, usually, become very defensive when I point out the similarities. They do not want anyone who is like their fathers, but their childhood pain blocks this awareness. One birth mother analyzed her relationships and found that all of them were very similar to her father. Her father had abandoned the family when she was only two years old. Her contact with him was sporadic, at best. When her dad remarried, he became somewhat more active in her life, but continued to have his own unresolved issues with alcohol. Her father had a pattern of avoiding dealing with any issues, at all cost, which included his daughter's self-esteem. It is impossible to be in a relationship with alcohol, to the extent that he was, and be in any healthy relationships simultaneously, because the alcohol numbs his feelings and assists in avoiding issues. When people are unaware of their feelings, they are also unaware of their own emotional needs and the needs of others. This situation has the potential to cause great harm to others, especially to children who see their parents as "god-like." In the previous example, this father was unaware of his daughter's needs and the important role he played in her life. A child's self-esteem first comes from his/her parents. As the child matures, she is then able to define her own, but usually not until her late teens or early twenties. This girl felt unimportant in her father's life since he did not place her on his priority list of things to do. Therefore, she believed that she was worthless in his eyes. That belief followed her into her teenage years where she encountered many boys who were "hormonally charged." She was so hungry for male attention that she sacrificed her own needs and sexual boundaries just for a moment of feeling "special." Of course, when the boys got what they were after, they became disinterested, which then reinforced her low opinion of herself. These issues were not hers, originally; they were her father's, but they had an enormous effect on his daughter, who now has taken her issues into young adulthood. Our focus in therapy has been on allowing God to define her self-esteem instead of men. If she can see herself through God's eyes, and if she can feel just how important she is to The Creator of the Universe, then she can heal.

News Flash: Now there is birth control!

I know that this is no big news to you and me, but birth control is seems to be unheard of with young people!

Jane Waters

My experience is that, most of the time, the girls use NO form of birth control whatsoever. And, the ones who do use it, use it only sporadically. Even the ones who had previous pregnancies think that they won't get pregnant a second time! This is an area that has me completely frustrated. Most teenagers, in general, think they are invincible creatures who are immune to consequences and, certainly, are outside of "nature's laws." If the girl is not in a relationship, then she believes, and accurately so, that birth control is unnecessary. It is, that is, until she finds herself in the back seat of a parked car with a boy who is telling her just how special she is! Alcohol is usually involved, which blurs her judgment and her ability to hold boundaries. Most of the girls tell me, though, that they just never think about it when they're in the situation. Most of the guys either do not think about it, or they assume that the girl is using birth control. They never engage in sex with the primary goal being pregnancy. "It just happens!" They are embarrassed to discuss it! They don't mind having sex, but they just don't want to talk about personal things like birth control! Teenagers' thought processes are not fully formed enough to be able to think through a situation like this one which has the potential for such devastating consequences. Sometimes, we adults do not seem to either!

Make a selection from the menu below

Pregnancy is not the only issue with which they are dealing. Most birth mothers are dealing with at least two or three issues. Some of the other issues with which they are dealing include drug and alcohol addiction, codependency, physical, sexual, or emotional abuse, ADD/ADHD, learning disabilities, spiritual bankruptcy, depression, bi-polar disorders, anxiety disorders, low self-esteem, unforgiveness, and homelessness to name just a few. Can you imagine trying to manage a mix of these while pregnant and trying to decide whether or not to parent? Overwhelming, to say the least! If a mood disorder is severe enough, often medication will be involved. A strong support system is needed in addition to therapy, mentoring, and medical care.

CHAPTER TWO: HOW OPEN DO YOU WANT TO GO?

One of the biggest decisions in considering open adoption is deciding how "open" you would like your adoption to be. There is no right or wrong answer on this. It's just a matter of knowing what you and your husband are called by God to do. You must be open and honest with yourself and with your spouse in this area, and you must be in prayer, too.

Most people are uneducated about open adoption, so don't be hesitant about finding out all you can about the differences between open and closed adoptions. Delve into books on open adoption, ask others who have been through the experience, and then search your own heart for which is right for you. Think of open adoption as a long continuum of choices, not just open or closed. Twice a year, the agency with which I work, offers a workshop for the awaiting families. When I speak to the group of couples on the expectations of birth mothers, one of the things I have them do is an experiential activity which helps give them an idea of the continuum of openness. I put a person on one end of the room who represents "just barely open," and, on the other side of the room, I place another person who represents "total openness/no holds barred." I ask the couples to place themselves somewhere in between the two ends which reflect their preference of openness. The couples tell me that they would have placed themselves in one place before the workshop, and another place afterwards. The change is, primarily, due to all the information they receive from testimonies of birth mothers, adoptive couples who have been through this process, the lawyer, the doctor. The couples tell me that, by the end of the workshop, they feel much more comfortable with the idea of openness, and more assured by the rewarding experiences that they hear. In the experiential exercise, most couples, initially, place themselves more towards the conservative end, but then, after hearing the testimonies, decide to move more towards the "more open" end. It doesn't matter where you "place" yourself on the continuum. What is most important is that you are aware of what your preference is, and that you honestly reflect that to others.

The birth mother's strongest need is to find the couple most similar to her preferences. The similarity in expectations and preferences is what makes for the most successful adoption. Some birth mothers only want contact in the form of pictures sent yearly. Some want contact only several times a year. Others want monthly, if not weekly visits, while keeping a close relationship with the adoptive mother, if they have become friends.

In my experience, the worst combination is when the birth mother wants much more contact than the adopting couple. In other words, that particular combination seems to produce the most heartache for the girl, and frustration for the adopting couple. The best combination is when the birth mother's range preference is the same as the couple's. Those seem to go smoothly, produce the most fruit, and be the most meaningful for everyone involved. The winner in all of this is the child. The baby is blessed by the easy-going, friendly, and respectful relationship between the birth mother and the adoptive couple. Even when the couple wants more contact than the birth mother, it does not produce the amount of problems as in the first scenario. The couple may be sad and disappointed in this case, but not the heartache as in the above case.

I've seen countless open adoptions over the years, which were attainable, fruitful, and, and very successful. If you hold yourself accountable to God and to each other, educate yourself on the process, and follow the instructions in this book, you have every reason to expect and enjoy your adoption. It's all worth it for the children!

CHAPTER THREE: OBSTACLES TO A SUCCESSFUL ADOPTION:

It is my experience that approximately 90% percent of the open adoptions that I've seen are successful, which I define as without significant problems that disrupt the adoption or which damage relationships. However, there is that 10% that do experience challenges to everyone. There may be others, but I've outlined several areas that produce the most problems.

Dishonesty

The number one reason for most of the difficulties in adoptions is dishonesty, whether intentional or unintentional. I need to be brutally honest and direct in this area and I encourage you to search out your heart on this one. By intentional dishonesty, I mean that a couple deliberately misrepresents themselves to the agency and to the birth mother in the hope of getting the child. This causes incredible damage to the birth mother. Some years ago, there was a couple who came to the agency and represented themselves as Christians interested in adoption. The woman was the one who did most of the talking in the interview with the director of the agency and with me in therapy. Her husband appeared passive and anxious. This woman was very clever and deceptive. She said all the "right things" and eventually was picked by a birth mother. Then, after the birth, they broke all their promises to the birth mother and to the agency. They intentionally misled everyone into believing that they truly cared about the birth mother and that she could see the baby often. In hindsight, we were able to clearly see that the woman had no intention of honoring those promises and showed no care at all for the girl who had given them the most precious gift of all. They refused to be forthright in dealings with me or the agency director. They eventually moved out of the area with no hint of where. Needless to say, the birth mother was devastated and it took months for her to recover from that event. That is one of the most extreme situations that we've seen, but even once is too much.

The more common situation that I've seen in this area is in the case of unintentional dishonesty. Couples in this category are not evil people who deliberately set out to hurt other people just to get what they want, as in the above case. This type of couple is afraid of trusting God to bring them a child, fearful of not being selected, or fearful of being disliked by the birth mother. For example, while being interviewed by the birth mother, an adoptive couple became somewhat uncomfortable. The birth mother was very talkative, excited, and dominated the conversation. The girl just stated her preferences without asking many questions of the couple. The couple had not even thought about some of the scenarios about which the girl asked. The couple did not speak up about their preferences, but stayed quiet and passive. After the birth of the baby, the adoptive mother found it more and more difficult to adhere to what was agreed upon for visiting, but was fearful to say anything. She kept her feelings to herself, which contributed to her growing resentment toward the birth mother, who was unaware that there was any problem. The damage in this case was minimal. We had a session with everyone involved where I encouraged each to be open and honest about their feelings. By the end of the session, everyone had a clearer picture of how the other one truly felt, and adjustments were made to accommodate their new understanding.

The solution is for you and your spouse to search your soul for your preferences and expectations for an adoption, to examine your faith in God, to stay in prayer during the entire process, and be open and honest with the agency and the birth mother. When you are fearful or anxious, always return to the Source of Comfort, Your Creator, and Your Provider. If His will is for you to be a parent, then He will make it come to pass. If The Almighty ordains it, it will happen. His timing is always best and He knows precisely which child you should have. Require yourself as a Christian adult to do these things, and you will see His glory. Remember that we are not only called to parent, we are called to minister to others, especially young, pregnant girls who are scared and even those who appear not to be.

Rigidity and Fear

If you are a Christian, then you already know that fear is not from God. It is when fear rises above the level of faith for the moment. But, instead of facing that issue in us when fear arises, we tend to focus outward onto other people's issues. Fear makes us rigid in our expectations, both of ourselves and others as well. This comes across as "controlling" behavior, which no one else really appreciates and can actually do much harm to relationships if the focus stays on the outward behavior instead of looking inwardly at the feelings. Some years ago, there was an adoptive couple who lived in a different state than the birth mother. During their discussions in her pregnancy, they had all agreed on three to four visits a year. At that time, the birth mother did not feel a need for more contact. After the birth of the baby, she felt differently. She wanted to have a little more contact than upon which they had agreed. The intensity of her own feelings towards the baby surprised her, so she asked if she could visit an extra time during the year. This was not a huge deviation from the original plan, but it caused fear in the adoptive couple. They were cautious, and then became rigid. The birth mother felt the couple distancing themselves, and became fearful. Fear told her that she would never get to see her child again, so she began to push for more visiting times. Well, you can guess how quickly it spiraled downhill for everyone. This was more difficult to resolve because the couple was out of state, but I made many phone calls to the couple. They were finally willing to allow one more visit, but the damage to the relationship had already been done and was now difficult to repair. Most of the adoptive couples are much more flexible than that, so this was a rare case. However, had the couple listened to the girl's needs, reassured her of her place of honor in their family, prayed about what Jesus wanted them to do, and showed compassion for her grief, I think the damage would have been minimal, if any.

Late Entrance Into The Adoption Agency

There are so many tasks to address during a girl's pregnancy and it requires time to be able to face them all. If a girl does not enter the agency until her ninth month, then she has little time to select the adoptive couple and even less time to develop a relationship with them. This leaves many emotional issues to be addressed only **after** the birth. Can you imagine trying to make the best decision possible for the child, dealing with your own grief issues, developing a trust with the agency and with the adoptive couple, and stabilizing the situation in only three weeks? Not impossible, but definitely not preferred. We address what we can before the birth, and then we face the emotional issues "after the fact." This can leave the birth mother guessing about whether or not she made the right decision, which would be torturous for her. One of the best things about open adoption for the birth mother is being able to have a relationship with the adoptive couple, which adds continuing reassurance that not only did she make the best decision, but that she also selected the couple she felt could best parent this child. That kind of comfort and peace of mind will see her through many tearful nights.

The ideal scenario is to have the birth mother enter the agency early in her pregnancy so that she can receive the greatest amount of benefits from the support group, therapy, and time it takes to face all of her decisions.

She can have all of her questions answered, play out all scenarios, and come to terms with issues while still having time to select the right couple, develop a relationship with them based on trust, love for God, and love for the baby, all before the baby is born.

The agency with which I work not only offers a greatly needed support group for the girls, but also pays for and adamantly supports counseling before, during, and after the birth for as long as they need it. Some girls even return sporadically when they face new issues or anniversary dates of the birth. The agency also provides mentors for each of the girls which increase their support system. Few agencies offer that, but those who do, promote the most successful adoptions.

Just as it is critical for the birth mothers to have a support system, so also must the adoptive couples. It's very common, especially for the adoptive mothers, to feel alone and unsure of what is expected of them during this time. Some have found it convenient to use the birth mother, who has chosen them, as their support system. It can be beneficial in the beginning of their relationship when each is getting to know the other and develop trust. However, if that is the main source of support for the adoptive mother, then that may cause problems after the baby is born. It's easy to get used to the daily contact they might have with each other with the excitement of the impending birth. I have seen many develop really close relationships with each other. By itself, this is not bad. However, realistically, most of the relationships change somewhat after the birth. It would be difficult for the adoptive mother to keep up the intensity of that relationship while caring for a newborn. That does not mean that her love for the birth mom would somehow lessen. It just means that she's going to be losing a lot of sleep, while trying to meet the needs of a demanding baby. It's normal for the focus to shift as well. Before the birth, typically the adoptive mother's focus is on the birth mother, then shifting to the baby afterwards. The adoptive mother must be sensitive to the feelings of the birth mother in this area. I've seen many girls with hurt feelings assuming that because the adoptive mothers are less involved in their lives that this means their love for them has diminished. In most cases, nothing could be further from the truth. It means that the adoptive mother is taking her role as new parent very seriously.

She wants to be a great parent and, in order to do that, she needs bonding time with the baby, which means she has fewer hours in a day or week to spend with the birth mother. In contrast, just as it is the most exciting time in your life, it is the most painful part of the birth mother's life. Sometimes, the birth mother needs time and space without contact from the adoptive couple as she heals, physically and emotionally. If the adoptive mother has depended upon the birth mother as her total support, and now the birth mother needs time to heal, then the adoptive mother will find herself without support, just at a time when she may need it the most.

Both women must be aware of the other's role in this transition, so that they may view the other in a new light. By doing this, each can be more detached and take things less personally so that there can be fewer hurt feelings. Their relationship must be redefined at this point. If it is not addressed, then each sets herself up for disappointment, hurt, and anger. Communication, prayer, compassion, and sensitivity to the other are essential ingredients to transition successfully, plus a strong support system for the adoptive mother through friends, family, church, therapy, and the support group for the adoptive parents if the agency has one.

Faith

This seems like a fairly obvious factor that would help make the adoption process more successful, but it warrants being said. Faith is the single most important ingredient in this mixture! By faith, I do not just mean only a belief in the existence of an all-knowing God in Heaven who is all powerful and Creator and one that you offer up prayers to in hopes that He'll listen. No, by faith, I mean a "relationship." Relationship is the key word. Knowing "about" the Lord is very different from "knowing" the Lord. This is a powerful distinction. If you don't have a relationship whereby you can be in conversation with the Lord, then how can you know His will for your life? If you don't know His will for you, then how will you know if or when it's His desire for you to become adoptive parents? We must, first, ask Our Creator, (you remember, the one with the Big Plans for the Universe,) if this is in His plan. If it is, then you can begin preparing for that to occur. If God promises it, then it will come to pass.

If He has ordained it for your life, then you can take comfort in knowing that He is "greasing" the path for this to occur. So, discernment about His will for you is of utmost importance before you prepare.

Of course, faith is important throughout your entire life, but it will have a powerful effect on the adoption process and how you minister to the birth mother. Remember that the birth mothers, quite frequently, face more issues than just pregnancy. One client of mine faced a drug addiction, depression, a severe codependency to males, and few social skills. Her life was chaotic and far from stabilized. Her parents did not have a stable home to offer her and her support system was nonexistent. She had a learning disability, which contributed to her low level of insight into her own feelings and behavior and those of others. Can you imagine how chaotic it would be for you, as the adoptive parent whom she chose, to face that situation without the focus of God, His Will for you, and not knowing how He wanted you to minister to her? It would seem impossible. Yet, I have seen the power of God work in a situation just as this, which produced fine fruit! This couple had a great relationship with the Lord, and made no big decisions without first consulting Him. God was their stability, their focus, their strength, and the only one from whom they took orders. One of the blessings in this "challenging" situation was that the couple had to stay so close to their Maker, that they could feel His whisper in their ears. Their love of God and trust in Him grew to levels they did not think possible, and the birth mother was blessed by this as well.

Grief Process

Grief comes with any transition. By definition, change means that something is gained, but something is lost as well in the process. Grief can be difficult to work through for anyone, but especially for the young adults. Facing the decision to make an adoption plan for their babies means that they will, to whatever degree, go through the grief process.

Kubler-Ross describes the grief process in her book, Death and Dying. She states that there are, typically, five stages of grief that people normally experience when there has been a loss. These stages are denial, anger, bargaining, depression, and then acceptance. This is applicable not only in situations where there has been a death, but also divorce, a job change, a wedding, the loss of a dream, and any situation where there is a transition, either positive or negative, including adoption.

Though these stages are predictable, the length and intensity of each is not. This is a very individualized process and must be treated accordingly. Most birth mothers spend a short amount of time in the denial stage. They take a pregnancy test and stare at the positive result for a long time, thinking that there is no way this could be happening. Others ask them if they are pregnant and they will categorically deny it. Denial results when emotions are overwhelming and intense, thus the need for compartmentalizing them until we can better deal with them. In rare instances, I have seen girls whose denial is so intact that they give birth without ever believing they are pregnant. However, in most cases, this stage lasts a relatively brief period of time.

When they emerge from denial, typically the girls feel anger. They are angry at anything and everything at this point. They are angry at the boyfriend, themselves, all men, the grocery clerk, and basically anything breathing. Actually, they can be angry at inanimate objects as well, like their car, schoolwork, lack of world peace. You get the picture. When anger is just beneath the surface, they are usually feeling fear deep inside, but rather than acknowledge the fear, it just comes out as irritability and anger. Anger is a "secondary" emotion and acts like a protective device for our more vulnerable emotions, like fear, hurt, or sadness. Anger is like the hard peanut shell on the outside which protects the more vulnerable peanut on the inside. Anger can, also, be the result of continued frustration which has not resolved itself. Plus, anger feels more empowering than fear or hurt. The energy behind the anger can actually help energize the girls into taking necessary action, like setting boundaries, and getting help, which is essential. For these reasons, anger can be very redeeming! This stage usually lasts longer than denial. It can last for days, months, and sometimes even years if the process gets stuck. Eventually, the birth mothers will have to face the anger they feel towards the adoptive couple for being able to parent when they cannot.

When the frustration and anger seem irresolvable, they will then begin to move into the bargaining stage. In this stage, the girls try to bargain with God about changing the pregnancy. I hear statements like, "I promise to go to church (or back to school) if God gets me out of this." Or, "I'll never run away again if God will make this all go away." There is a desperation and plea to God Almighty in this stage. The reality of pregnancy is too overwhelming, and they will do anything if somebody will just change it. This stage, like denial, is shorter than the others.

One of the most common stages in this process is depression. When a birth mother can no longer deny her pregnancy, when she faces all the reactions from family and friends, and when the bargaining has not changed anything, she can slip into a depression. Unlike anger, depression has no energy to it. Depression is filled with hopelessness and helplessness for her. She feels forgotten by God, judged by friends, and, sometimes, shut out by family. She feels alone. She has searched for a way and can't make a way soon enough to be able to parent. Despair is large and looming. Most girls spend the longest amount of time in this stage. Sometimes medication is needed to thwart suicidal thoughts and to quiet the endless days of tears. It is heart wrenching to watch these young girls fumble their way through this. It's not a pretty stage and feels endless.

Just when the girls think that there is no end to the darkness, light appears. It appears in the form of acceptance. Acceptance is a wonderfully relieving feeling. When a birth mother is in this stage, she releases the constant battle and resulting battle fatigue, and hope emerges. She is ready to face reality with a clarity that she had never before experienced. And it feels good. This does not happen on its own; rather, it's a result of prayer. It comes in the form of peace sent directly from our Heavenly Father who has not left her side for one moment. He has counted every tear. God has heard her prayers and He gives her peace as He guides her to the couple whom He has chosen to parent her child. Her relationship with the adoptive couple grows. Her trust in the Lord grows and faith is strengthened. All is good in this stage.

The problem is not that the girls go through these stages. The problem is that the adoptive couples don't know that this is a grief process. When I explain this to the birth mothers and the couples, they are relieved to know that this is normal. They welcome any information on this. It helps put a "picture frame" around the entire "scene." Rather than focus on every single incident, mood, or word said, they can step back and look at the entire picture and identify it as grief. When they can identify which stage she's in, they will have a clearer understanding of how they need to minister to her.

It's challenging enough if one person is experiencing grief. Think how much more difficult it would be if the adoptive couple were going through this as well! One adoptive mother had just lost her own mother soon after she was selected by a birth mom. Can you imagine the grief she went through during a time that was supposed to be joyous? Keeping track of one person's grief is hard enough, but two? Just as the birth mom would be in the anger stage, the adoptive mom would be in a deep depression. The girl misinterpreted the depression to mean that the adoptive mother was just not excited about being selected to parent. We had many sessions during this time with everyone present, focusing on feelings and communication. Doing this with a third party present allowed everyone to see the situation from a more detached viewpoint, which greatly improved the process for everyone. "Life" happens during the pregnancy and impending birth, and it certainly continues to happen afterwards. So, remember to be aware of the bigger picture for all parties involved.

My own personal opinion is that the grief process is not complete until we have reached forgiveness. Why settle for mere acceptance when forgiveness can offer us so much more? We as Christians have no choice but to face this daunting task because it is what we are called to do. Usually the birth mother finds that there are many people whom she needs to forgive like the boyfriend, family members, friends, possibly God and, most importantly, herself. Some are easier to forgive than others, but we are only as sick as our "unforgiveness," so we must address this. When I was asked by a birth mother why she had to forgive the one who date-raped her, I responded, "Because that is what we, as Christians, are called to do. It is a requirement." This girl wondered if God was aware of what He was asking her to do! More than anyone else, our Creator knows exactly that which He is calling us to do. He is the Creator of forgiveness. After all, He was the One who sent His Son to die for us! He watched what we did to His Son, and He forgave. So, He knows what He is asking us to do.

I further explained that forgiveness affects our personal health standpoint. If we do not forgive, we keep all the anger, resentment, and hurt wrapped around our hearts, which prevents warmth from getting in or out. We become guarded, defensive, and distrustful of others, which affects our psychological health, physical health, self-esteem, and relationships.

Forgiveness is difficult, but very rewarding. In his article, "Forgiving: the healing secret," Lewis B. Smedes, Ph.D., said, "Forgiving is love's toughest work. But you can make it easier if you don't confuse forgiving with forgetting. You do not have to forget in order to forgive. Besides, some things should never be forgotten, lest we let them happen again." Smedes agrees with the statement that some people don't deserve to be forgiven. In his article, he asks the reader, "If you've been hurt, do you deserve to go on hurting? Or do you, instead, deserve to be healed?"

The small offenses are easier to forgive than the huge ones. Most of us can forgive others for minor offenses. But, what about the biggest ones? For these, there is only one way to do it: through God. When we do not **want** to forgive, He can give us the desire and willingness. You may wonder why we would want to hold onto the anger at those who have harmed us. There are several reasons. The first is that we have a misperception of forgiveness. We erroneously believe that if we release our anger, we're saying that the infraction was not that big. We, also, may believe that if we forgive, then the person will not get his "just" punishment. Somehow we believe that our anger would be their punishment for the offense. It is not. The anger only serves to suffocate and destroy us. Even worse, when we hold our anger tightly, then we are, in an odd sense, honoring the very one who offended us!

Great things can, and do, happen when we place the Cross between us and the ones who have harmed us. When we see the person through the **Cross**, we see them as though we were looking through Jesus' eyes. Jesus **is** love and forgiveness. He saves us from ourselves and from each other. He knows what it's like to be harmed, betrayed, repeatedly hurt by strangers and loved ones; yet He forgave. So, it is **because** the offense is huge that we must involve Him. We, alone, would not be able to do it. When you involve Him, expect a miracle! Expect to move on with your life and be thankful because the life lived in forgiveness is blessed!

CHAPTER FOUR: FORGIVENESS

In an earlier chapter, I mentioned forgiveness as one of the biggest issues with which the birth mothers face. It is such a critical part of the therapy process that I decided to devote an entire chapter to it. A word of warning though: if *you* have any unresolved issues, reading this may be difficult. If you have been wounded in childhood or adulthood by people whom you have trusted and you have not addressed it, you may find that God is calling you to face these wounds now. Where there is unforgiveness, there is distance from God. I believe that God uses any realm (in this case, adoption) to deepen our relationship with Him. He needs us to be wholly and holy healed so that we can do His work on earth. Additionally, unhealed areas always interfere with relationships. You are about to enter into one of the most significant relationships of your life. You can use this time to address these areas so that the relationship with your birth mother will be as successful as possible. Two unhealed people in a relationship can mean a formula for disaster!

This chapter will also help you to understand what these girls have been through and how its effect on them. Knowing this will help you minister to them in a way that would be healing for them. Many of the birth mothers whom I have seen have been sexually, physically, emotionally abused or neglected by people whom they trusted. One birth mother had been sexually abused by her alcoholic step-father in the fifth grade which lasted four years. Her mother worked long hours outside the home and trusted the step-father to care for her daughter. The girl was afraid to tell her overly-burdened and exhausted mother, thinking that telling her would contribute to her problems. To make matters worse, her biological father left when she was a baby and had only sporadically contacted her since. The birth mother felt alone, hopeless, and depressed for years. In the ninth grade, she began to drink. She discovered that alcohol temporarily made her problems disappear. Under the influence, she felt strong, energized, empowered, and accepted by new "friends" who had introduced her to this lifestyle. One night while she and her friends were out partying, she met a young man who was eighteen. He was nice, kind, and friendly to her, which made her feel special. After secretly dating for two weeks, they became sexually involved. She was hesitant, but he made her feel so special and even told her that he loved her so she gave in. Because of her childhood issues involving the fathers in her life, she falsely believed that her feelings weren't important and that she should just submit to his pressure. She became pregnant within a few weeks. Her boyfriend suddenly began calling her less, eventually breaking up with her. He blamed her for the pregnancy and said he was not in a place where he wanted to parent. He never called again. She was fourteen, alone, and pregnant. Her mother and step-father became angry when she told them but took her to Crisis Pregnancy Outreach out of desperation. There they found hope, support, and a lovely couple anxious to adopt her baby. The adoption went very well, but the birth mother found she was filled with bitterness, resentment, and anger towards all who had betrayed and hurt her. The focus of therapy became forgiveness. The adoption allowed her to proceed with her life plan, but healing of these issues was needed so that she could emotionally do so as well. She needed information and understanding of forgiveness, God, therapy, and support to help her achieve this.

Forgiveness can be difficult, but very rewarding. First, though, it's beneficial to define what forgiveness is not. In their article, "Forgiven," Simon and Simon succinctly state what forgiveness is and what it is not.

Forgiveness is not:

- Forgiveness is not forgetting
- Forgiveness is not condoning
- Forgiveness is not absolution
- Forgiveness is not a form of self-sacrifice
- Forgiveness is not a clear-cut, one-step decision
- Forgiveness is not an indication that you trust the other person

- Forgiveness is not dependent upon the other person

Forgiveness is:

- Forgiveness is an act of the will, not of the emotions
- Forgiveness is a sign of positive self-esteem
- Forgiveness is a by-product of an ongoing healing process
- Forgiveness is accepting that nothing we do to punish them will heal us
- Forgiveness is to be developed into a lifestyle
- Forgiveness is required of a Christian

In an article called "Forgiven," authors Sidney B. Simon and Suzanne Simon even state that "not forgiving provides you with certain payoffs or illusions." This first illusion is "if this hadn't happened, you'd have a 'perfect' life. "Not forgiving provides an available explanation or excuse for anything and everything that is wrong with you and your life." It's too easy to maintain false beliefs, which are really fantasy thoughts. One birth mother explained that had she not been abused by her grandfather, then she would have been an outgoing, vibrant young woman who could have "made it" in the theatre. Maybe that is true, or maybe it's not, but she used it as a crutch to avoid her fear of failure as well as taking responsibility for her own behavior and choices, as a young adult.

Simon and Simon describe another illusion: that of being "good." They state that "not forgiving helps you define who you are: You are the victim of some injury or injustice." The author believe that this belief provides the person some amount of comfort that you are one of the "good guys" and the ones who hurt you are the "bad guys," and that "once you forgive, the world can never again be defined in such black-and-white terms." In this scenario, the focus is on us being the victim. In reality, we hurt others, too. We need forgiveness just as much as we need to forgive. The focus needs to be on God and what He would have us do. If God calls us to forgive and He always does then we need to be obedient. Just as we can focus on being the victim, there are others who believe that they've done things so horribly that they cannot be forgiven. This view also focuses on self, rather than God. Remember, He is the One who defines who we are. We are the ones who must accept His grace. If we do not, then we do not hold Him as Lord, and we hold *our* opinion as more important than *His*. This reality often serves as a "divine two by four upside the head," a phrase that my husband uses to refer to times when God wants to get our attention.

The biggest "pay-off" for not forgiving is the illusion of power. We've all been there, haven't we? It feels powerful when we are in the position of the one **doing** the forgiving, or, more accurately, withholding forgiveness. This is a distorted use of power. When we refuse to forgive, we have the potential of becoming self-righteous, indignant, and judgmental, which is not a good combination if we want to "win friends and influence people!" Simon and Simon state that "not forgiving helps you compensate for the powerlessness you felt when you were hurt." However, our source of power needs to come, not from ourselves, but from the One who made us. When we are obedient to His call and His timing, then His mighty power pours grace not only on us, but on others, as well. It's His Spirit that allows for true healing and getting our hearts right again, which readies us to do more of His work.

The last illusion that we have if you choose not to forgive, according to Simon and Simon, is that "you won't be hurt again." They state that "by keeping the pain alive and your guard up, you reduce the risk of ever again being rejected, deceived, abused, betrayed or otherwise injured." Of course, nothing could be further from the truth! Your walls are the very thing that keeps people at a distance, which only serves to make us lonely. The walls make us appear unapproachable, cold-hearted, arrogant, or mean, which is not particularly attractive to others! The goal is to heal so that we can do God's work and minister to others. We can't do that if we are seeing only what people can give or do for us, rather than what we can do for or give to others. Think how different the world would be if all of us would adhere to that belief! I agree with Simon and Simon when they say that "the life you have now and can keep by not forgiving is not nearly as full and fulfilling as the life you could create by letting go of the pain and making peace with the past." Forgiveness leads to true freedom and total dependence on God, which is always what He has in mind. The wounds, then, can actually be blessings in disguise because they make us turn to Him constantly. In so doing, our trust and faith in Him build and helps establish a firm relationship on which we can stand in painful as well as joyful times.

I believe that it is easy for us to get into the habit of not forgiving. This allows us to take the easy way out. We can avoid our own issues, while blaming others for theirs. However, this only manages to keep us stagnant in our bitterness. We, then, become critical and negative people around whom nobody wants to be, which hurts us even further.

Sometimes, complete forgiveness happens overnight, but mostly, it is a process by which the birth mother will have to forgive and re-forgive on a daily basis. In the above-mentioned article, authors Sidney Simon and Suzanne Simon believe that there are stages of forgiveness. They state that the first stage is denial. "This is the stage in which we attempt to play down the impact or importance of painful past experiences." The second stage is self-blame, when we "try to explain what happened to us by assuming we were somehow responsible for the injuries and injustices we suffered, decimating our self-esteem as we work overtime to convince ourselves that we would not have been hurt if only we had been different or had done things differently." The third stage is "victim." In this stage, Simon and Simon state that "we recognize that we did not deserve or ask for the hurt we received," and that this is when we are "all aware of how much we were damaged by painful experiences, so much so that we wallow in self-pity, expect little of ourselves, indulge ourselves at the expense of those around us, or lash out at everyone and anyone who crosses us." The fourth stage, indignation, occurs when "we are angry at the people who hurt us and at the world. We want people who hurt us to pay and suffer as we have. Our tolerance is virtually nonexistent, and our self-righteousness is at an all-time high." The fifth stage, survivor, happens when we "recognize that although we were indeed hurt, we did in fact survive." It is when we realize that "our painful experiences took things away from us, but gave us things as well. We become aware of our strengths and welcome the return of our compassion, sense of humor and interest in matters other than the pain." The final stage is "integration." This is the stage in which "we are able to acknowledge that the people who hurt us may have been doing the best they could too; that if we are more than our wounds, they must be more than the inflictors of those wounds." These stages parallel, but are not identical to, the grief stages. Like grief, these are not clear cut, linear stages, but, as Simon and Simon point out, our hope is in knowing that our "healing process began the instant we were hurt." Our responsibility is to complete the process, with God's help, and maybe with the help of a therapist!

CHAPTER FIVE: BOUNDARIES

The dictionary on my computer gives several definitions of the word "boundary." The first definition uses it as a border, or an official line that divides one area of land from another. The second defines it as a "limit," the point at which something ends or beyond which it becomes something else, or the pushing back the boundaries of human knowledge.

I am, often, asked by potential adoptive parents if it's appropriate to have boundaries with the girls. My answer is always the same: "OH, MY, YES!" It is, also, appropriate and necessary for the girls to set appropriate boundaries with the adoptive families. I love boundaries because they help protect each person involved, and, also, the relationships. Without boundaries, no relationship would be healthy. If we choose not to set boundaries with others, then we are actively contributing to the damage and eventual demise of our relationships.

Part of the first definition describes a boundary as an official line that divides one area from another, referencing land, but we can apply it to ourselves and to our relationships. This "official line" helps us to know where one person begins and another person ends. It actually defines a person's job description, which is always helpful in clarifying one's role in a situation.

The second definition uses the word "limit," as in beyond a point where one thing becomes something else. This fits nicely when we talk about adoption. An adoptive parent does not carry the baby in her womb; but during and after birth, that person becomes, or transitions into, the parent. In a similar way, the birth mother, at some point, transitions into a non-parental role. Without that transition, there would be mass chaos. The transition is one of the most difficult processes that the birth mother will have to tackle. Some birth mothers will have little difficulty with this, but most will have to go through a period of "letting go." It's basically a grief process for them. They must come to terms with the fact that they will not be parenting, and therefore will have no control over how the child will be parented, where the family will live, with what activities the child will become involved, nor the one whom the child will call "Mom." As with the grief process, there is no definite period of time that this takes. Some birth moms will begin that process during pregnancy, and others will not start until after the baby's birth. This has the potential of complicating the relationship between the birth mom and the adoptive couple. It will take both compassion and boundaries, from the couple, to help her through this process. It's very important for the girl to stay involved with therapy and the support group, which will give her strength, understanding, and support as long as she needs it. These services are absolutely invaluable, but most adoptive agencies do not offer this. CPO believes in taking care of the birth mothers' emotional needs for as long as necessary. In some cases, the services will only be needed for a few weeks. In other cases, it may take months before they are comfortable with the transition, although anniversary dates of the child's birth and Mother's Days may bring up unresolved issues. Remembering them, especially on these dates, is vitally important. Send her a picture or a card; call her; take her out to lunch. These are just a few ways in which you can honor the person who gave you the biggest gift and your heart's desire.

This does not mean that open adoption causes the confusion. It means that when there is no distinction between those roles, then there will be problems.

Let me give you some examples of the problems that a lack of boundaries can cause. One adoptive couple I worked with wanted to please their birth mother, having a great deal of compassion for her and wanting not to be the cause of any emotional pain for her, especially after the birth. Because of that, they allowed the birth mother to come over every day and stay for as long as she liked. Then, when she went home, she called the couple several times in the evening. The couple didn't want her to feel rejected, so they put no limitations on that. In the process, they became physically and emotionally drained and began to resent the birth mother. The sad part was not that there was too much contact with the birth mother, but that the adoptive couple did not respect their own needs and gave more than they had the ability to give. Their lack of boundaries caused problems between everyone. Some adoptive mothers thrive off of having people around all the time, while others don't. We solved the problem pretty quickly by having everyone in the therapy session with me to discuss feelings openly and to initiate some basic ground rules and limitations. The birth mother willingly agreed because she wanted (actually needed) the adoptive mom to be physically and emotionally rested so that she could parent the child that the birth mother had just relinquished to her. Boundaries protected the adoptive couple and saved the relationship between them and their birth mother.

Just as too few boundaries can cause damage, so can too many boundaries. For example, before the baby was due, another adoptive couple and birth mother met with me to discuss expectations of each other both during and after the birth. They agreed on the amount and type of contact they would have with each other. After the baby was born, the birth mother was surprised by the intensity of her feelings and wanted to have more contact with the baby than they had discussed. The adoptive couple immediately became rigid and seemed to honor "the rule" more than the birth mother and her needs. Underlying their rigidity was fear that she would change her mind and take back the child. As is often the case when any of us feels fear, we also feel a loss of control, which then makes us more controlling and rigid. As the adoptive couple began to pull away, the birth mother's fear of never seeing her child again began to intensify. With fear increasing, she, too, became very controlling and demanding. When the couple and birth mother met with me, we focused on feelings of loss, sadness, and fear. Having the couple's feelings understood allowed their fears to decrease. As their fear decreased, they found themselves able to be more flexible in their contact with the birth mother. The birth mother responded quickly to their flexibility and became much less demanding. With the couple's compassion, the support group, and therapy, the birth mother was able to resolve her grief issues and move on. Fear on either side, if not handled well, can freeze the grieving process for the birth mother which, in turn, has the potential to cause problems.

As demonstrated, either end of the boundary continuum can cause problems. It's healthiest to have boundaries, but to also be flexible as needs arise. Communication and prayer play vital roles in this situation. When both the adoptive couple and birth mother derive their strength and foundation from their faith in and relationship with the Lord, the process has a much greater chance of being successful for everyone. When we see the bigger picture from our Heavenly Father's perspective, then we can experience more compassion and healing. Adoption provides another opportunity for all involved to deepen our relationship with Jesus. If we can require more of ourselves as Christian adults, then we can take this opportunity to represent (re-present) Christ to the birth mothers, which allows healing, joy, and peace for them and for ourselves. Is there anything more important than doing God's work? If God brings us TO something, then He will get us THROUGH it. God's plan and timing is always best.

CHAPTER SIX: THE HOSPITAL EXPERIENCE

One of the biggest issues that birth mothers must consider is that of the hospital experience. Even though this experience is relatively short, typically between one to seven days, it is one of the most important ones to face. There is no right or wrong way to do this, only preferences. Every birth mother should develop her own "birth plan," which includes how she will get to the hospital, who will be in the labor and delivery room with her, and what kind of contact she would like to have with the baby while there.

There are several reasons why this is such an important decision. The first is because for some mothers, this may be the only time that they will spend time with their baby. One birth mother selected an adoptive couple who lived in Europe. She, specifically, chose a couple who lived far away because she did not want to have much contact with the child. So, it was vital for this birth mother to have the optimum hospital experience. Another birth mother selected a couple who lived several states away, limiting her contact with the baby and the adoptive couple. Even the girls who select couples in the same area must do everything possible to have a successful hospital experience because it will be the only one they will have with this child.

The second reason is because this experience will affect their grief process and subsequent emotional health. One birth mother, who entered the program in her final month of pregnancy, did not have much of an opportunity to analyze her own preference, nor did she have a lot of time to match her preference with the adoptive couple. By the time she came in for a session several weeks after the birth, she had become aware of how many regrets she had about the experience. She was sad because of how little time she spent alone with the baby, and was frustrated at the confusion of who was supposed to be in the labor room with her.

Subsequently, there were irritation and friction between the adoptive couple and her. This stunted her grief process because she was focused on the details of the experience, rather than on her feelings about the baby.

The hospital experience is vitally important to the adoptive couple. It can be a very stressful, anxious, and fearful experience for both parties. This is a time when reality hits the birth mother, and she can become overwhelmed with the intensity of her feelings of love for the baby, especially if this is her first pregnancy and birth. The intensity of her sadness or anger can surprise her as well. It is quite normal for the birth mother to consider parenting the child herself, even when she knows she can't. It is normal to hear such statements from her as, "I won't be able to go through with this," and, "I didn't know I would love her so much." **I repeat**, **this is normal**! It's an important part of the grief process. She will replay options and, usually, remind herself of the factors that made her choose adoption in the first place. It may take five minutes or it may take several days, but usually logic takes over within a few hours of the birth. Remember, she also has dramatically changed hormone levels, which cause **any** birth mother to experience mood swings. I am explaining all of this to you so that you can be prepared for what might happen in the hospital. It can be very painful for the adoptive couple to hear those comments and to fear she may change her mind. One couple I saw a few years ago was especially sensitive to this because they had experienced two previously failed adoptions, and were fearful of a third. If you are choosing adoption, you must face the risk as well. Be assured, however, that this only happens in a very small percentage of adoptions. Most birth mothers are just overwhelmed by the moment and adjust pretty quickly.

The hospital experience is important for the adoptive couple and the birth mother. You'll want to become clear on your own preferences and see how successfully they can match the birth mother's. The more similar they are, the better the hospital experience. Remember to be honest with yourself and your spouse about your preferences. Don't just agree in order to avoid a confrontation or out of fear that the birth mother won't be happy. Honest and open communication, with some flexibility when possible, is always the best ingredient of a successful hospital experience. I have provided a list of questions in Appendix A at the end of this book for you, your spouse, and the birth mother to answer and share with each other, which may help you become clear on your own preferences.

CHAPTER SEVEN: NAME THIS CHILD

Who gets to name this child? There is not a clear-cut answer. There are three choices. The first choice is that the adopting couple can chose the name. The second choice is that the birth mother can choose. The third option is that both can contribute.

This issue needs to be addressed with everyone because it can be a divisive one, if mishandled. In my practice, I have seen it work very successfully in all three scenarios. Sometimes, the adoptive couples feel strongly that they want to give that privilege to the birth mother. They want her to feel honored in that way, and do not have a need to be the only ones to name the child. That does not mean that the couples who want to name the child do not want to honor the birth mother.

It means that couples have different ways of showing respect and love for her. In the same way, some birth mothers want to honor the adopting couple by allowing them to name the child. The girls tell me that they feel such gratitude and love for the couple that they want to give them the honor. In both instances, neither have a pressing desire to be the one to offer a name. The third scenario seems to be the one which is most utilized, especially when there is a close relationship between the birth mother and the adoptive couple. In the excitement of anticipating the birth, the birth mother and adoptive mother will discuss their preferences for names. This is an area that can be fun for both. Brainstorming names can be a bonding experience. Each gets to know the preferences of the other and the ones they might have in common. Many times, one will choose the first name and the other will choose the middle name. Usually there is only a problem when one becomes rigid. This can be a potential area of conflict if you're set on one name only, and there is a pressing need to be the one to name the child.

If there are problems in the relationship between the two parties, it can show up in this area. If one party has been domineering, and the other one resents it, but says nothing, then that has the potential for conflict. This can be successfully addressed in therapy. The root of the disagreement can be examined and respected, which is very healing for the party. If the teenage girl particularly rebellious, she might disagree with any choice of names just for the sake of disagreement. On the other hand, I have seen an adoptive father be so insistent on naming the child after himself that he alienates his wife and the girl in the process. This particular man was insensitive to the feelings of the two most important women in his life. His pride and some childhood issues were the root of this demanding behavior. When discussed openly in therapy, it became a vehicle for healing these issues in himself and repaired the damage to the relationships.

CHAPTER EIGHT: WHAT ADOPTING PARENTS WANT YOU TO KNOW

To complete this book, I wanted to offer a particular point from the adopting couples' perspective. Over the years, I have met with many couples who had already adopted children or were awaiting selection. They all have many things in common, and are worth mentioning.

The first is that most of the adopting couples attend a support group which is offered by the agency with whom I've worked. What strikes me as fascinating is how many fathers attend! Keep in mind that my therapy work with the birth mothers rarely includes the birth fathers. Sadly, I can count on one hand the number of young men who are still involved with the birth mother and willing to participate in counseling! I always encouraged them to attend our sessions, with the birth mother's permission and willingness. However, most men do not want to get within twenty yards of a therapist's office and if, by some supernatural force they did attend, are hesitant to share anything especially *feelings*! So, you can understand why I am so pleased that many of the adoptive fathers attend. Not only do the fathers attend, they all share, quite willingly and enthusiastically! Most fathers have reservations, at first, about an open adoption, but most were changed by the healthy and healing experience of it, and are now strong proponents of open adoption.

When I attended the support group, I was most impressed at how the fathers held their babies! I wished several times that evening that I had brought my camera, so that I could capture the sights of men holding their tiny newborns in their big, strong hands and giving them little butterfly kisses on their soft faces. The adoptive mothers were no less photogenic when they held their "dreams" in their arms, while staring into their baby's faces and drinking up every line and contour.

A well-facilitated support group has members who minister to each another. The support group should be relaxed with a supportive atmosphere. Groups can grow to as large as thirty-five. It's rare for people to share on an intimate level, when you get a group of that size, but they can! Adoptive parents can be cheerleaders to the ones who were awaiting "that miracle phone call" informing them that they had just been selected by a birth mother to parent her child. The couples can share advice, listen intently, cry, and laugh together. When one meeting I attended was over, the couples did not rush out of the room praising God that the end of group had arrived! On the contrary, they continued to chat, listen, offer support, and laugh.

In support groups, there should be more "long-timers" present than new couples, which makes the atmosphere rich with wisdom and experience, giving hope to the waiting couples. In this agency's support group, most of the couples have at least one adoption through this agency, and have been attending this support group for months, if not years. At one meeting, two couples shared their experiences of living through two failed adoptions, explaining their emotional roller coaster of feelings and how they had healed with God's help. The waiting couples listened intently while others shared their experiences of going through the home studies, how they prepared for the baby before being selected, and how they had come to learn about patience. At that same meeting, I laughed when the long-timers chimed in together saying, "Get the car seat now!" Many laughed, remembering how it was with their adoption. Several had not expected to be called so soon and others had been called by the director saying, "We've had a drop-in birth mother at the hospital that just gave birth and wants to make an adoption plan; come get your baby!" One waiting adoptive mother was in another state at the time of the phone call. She laughed as she explained how she just dropped everything, got in the car, and sped (yes, sped) to the hospital, arriving only hours after the birth of the baby. Each couple seemed to tell their individual stories with fondness and respect. Everyone spoke with great humility and gratitude about being selected for receiving life's most precious gift. They spoke of their love for their birth mother and how courageous she was for choosing a good life for their baby. Some couples have adoptions that are complicated and difficult, but I am in awe that, when they ask for prayers for the birth mother, it is that she be given peace and strength to do God's will in her life.

The most painful thing that some couples deal with is the inconsistent contact from the birth mother, especially when the children become so attached to her. It is when the birth mother has been regularly and consistently involved with the baby and the other members of the adopted family, that her disappearance, for whatever reason, is disruptive and painful for the family. Her disappearance may be due to grief issues, addiction problems, or just continuing with her own life, all which are not unusual and expected. But, sometimes it is confusing and painful to the family. They only want the birth mother to be healthy, healed, involved, and happy.

One thing that is often mentioned by adoptive parents is the hospital experience, which can be the most intense time of the whole adoption process! One father at a support group meeting said, "God will provide opportunities during this time that will test you." His point was that Satan is present at all times, and would love to intervene in this most blessed time by distracting, confusing, and lying. So, his warning was, "Be prepared!" During the time at the hospital, God needs you to be focused on prayer, the birth mom, and the baby. Nothing is more important than these things and acknowledging God's hand and plan in all of this. Remember that you are one of the few people present who are non-hormonal at this time! As one adoptive mother put it so eloquently at a support group meeting, "Every birth comes with pain and stretch marks – so, too, it is for the adopting couple."

There may be times at the hospital when you find opportunities to minister to someone in need who needs a kind smile or word of encouragement. One adoptive father's comment was, "You never know who you can minister to at the hospital." He said that while they were waiting for labor to progress, he found an opportunity to listen to a man who was in need and each felt blessed by their conversation. Had the adoptive father been caught up in confusion, chaos, and drama, he would have missed that opportunity. Along the same lines, many adoptive couples have enthusiastically said, "Be nice to the nurses!" They all acknowledged that the nurses were trying to meet the needs of everyone present, which can get overwhelming at times. The hospital time is *not* the time to be selfish or focused on your own needs. It is the time to be the birth mom's advocate and getting that blessed miracle into this world, into an environment of peace, joy, and love!

Another stressful time for the adoptive couples is the time the birth mom's consent and the post-adoption visits. The consent process is the time when the birth mother legally relinquishes her rights to parent her baby. She stands before a judge and answers questions like, "Is this of your own free will?" The judge must be convinced that the birth mother is of sound mind and that she knows exactly what it means to choose adoption. This is a critical moment for both the birth mother and the adoptive parents. It's all on the line at this point, so this time can be very stressful. I know from my therapy sessions, that this can be a time when she finally understands the full ramifications of relinquishment. To the birth mom, it means that she has no control over how this child will be parented, where they will live, whether this child will be involved with school activities, sports, or even what she eats. For a few, this may be the first moment she steps out of denial and into the reality of the situation. However, the adoptive couple need not panic. For healing to occur, the birth mother must transition through this, which may mean that she'll feel grief, loss, sadness, and anger again, but remember that these grief feelings are normal and necessary for healing to occur. The couple may be fearful that she'll change her mind about the adoption, or that she will regret selecting them, which could cause their hair to turn white! Many adoptive parents said that this time was very anxiety-producing for them. But, they further said that this was just another opportunity to practice faith, focus, and a chance to show compassion to the person who would give them the greatest gift of their lives! Oklahoma law states that the birth mother cannot change her mind after she has formally relinquished her rights, which also helps relieve any anxiety the couple might be feeling. Be sure to check the laws in your state on this issue.

There is a psychological impact of the finalization process on the adopting couple, which takes place six to nine months after the birth of the baby. This formal proceeding somehow validates to the couple that they are, in fact, parents to this child. They may have felt that before this time, but some couples feel that this legal moment empowers them to be fully and solely the parents of this baby. This process entitles you to be seen by the world as the parents, and that you have every right to be called "mom" and "dad." Feeling this shift allows the couple to fully embrace the responsibilities and enjoyment of parenting, which they may have felt hesitant to feel to its fullest extent before this process.

Some adopting couples find their highest-anxiety producing moments to be during the post-placement visits. The agency employs a social worker who evaluates the couple through three visits at one, three, and five month intervals. The purpose of these visits is to determine if this was a successful placement. In my sessions and at the support group, I have heard just how nerve-wracking these visits can be. They must prove that the baby is thriving in their home environment and that all is as it should be in the best of circumstances. One couple said that this process made them feel like they were under a microscope. If the visits do not go well, then the baby may return to the agency. It can be a little unnerving to know that someone, who is basically unfamiliar with you, is analyzing your home, skills, and progress, to decide if you are a fit parent! One adoptive mother said that this process triggered feelings of inadequacy within her. She explained that, because of her own past issues, she feared that the agency would find that she was not good enough to parent! But, these were only issues of the past haunting her. Satan uses our issues as opportunities to lie to us, so don't give him the satisfaction of thinking you even noticed his comments! The only people that I know who are under this kind of scrutiny are famous stars and politicians! Further, in this society, a fourteen-year-old girl, who is unstable, addicted to methamphetamine, and without any parenting skills at all, can elect to parent without even being questioned or evaluated! It may seem unfair for a stable, married couple, who have spent years preparing and yearning for a child, be put through such an evaluation. Remember, though, that the agency is supportive of you and wants this to be successful. They are not trying to catch you doing something wrong; they just want to know that parents and baby are bonding and that she is being raised in a healthy and loving environment.

Lastly, I want to mention that people who are unfamiliar with adoption may say things that could be placed under the category of "Insensitive comments that you may hear from others!" This can occur anytime we are uncomfortable in a situation, which is mainly due to inexperience. For example, what does one say to a mother whose daughter has been raped? What does one say to a child whose father was murdered? We all make social blunders and it is no different in the case of adoption. One couple explained that they were shopping with their bi-racial adopted children, when a woman came up to them and asked if "they had any children of their own?" Frankly, I would have been appalled and speechless if I would have been asked that question, but this mother had a wonderful sense of humor that helped her cope with ignorant comments. When this mother told the story at a support group, another father suggested they respond to the rude woman by saying, "Nope, I just borrowed them for awhile!" Another rude comment came from a woman talking to the parents of another bi-racial child. She said, "I'm so glad she's at least light skinned!" Now, isn't that an odd thing to say? Did that woman think the parents wanted to hide that she was bi-racial? This particular couple chose to believe that the motivation behind the insensitive comment was that of care and concern for the parents, not to disrespect the child. These experiences are shared at the support group and can make it easier to cope. It makes a world of difference when you have a large support system that understands open adoption experiences, and can give you fresh perspectives and encouragement during the painful times.

Mainly, it just all boils down to loving yourself, your child, and others as Jesus loves us; with infinite patience, compassion, and forgiveness. Adoption will give you opportunities to choose the higher road of reflecting this. The Bible states it more clearly: love the Lord with all your heart, mind, and soul; love your neighbor as yourself!

A FINAL NOTE

Being an adoptive parent is one of the most rewarding, challenging, and important roles you will ever take on in your life. There will be times of great elation and times of deepest despair. The love you have for your child will know no greater depths, nor darkest heartache. These feelings do not, however, come from the adoption process, but from being a parent.

There are suggestions in this book that I hope you'll think about and apply, when necessary, to your situation. This can help make the adoption process much more manageable. No situation is perfect, nor should we expect it to be. We are not perfect, nor should we expect the birth mothers to be. If we are Christians, however, then we must hold ourselves accountable to a higher standard of behavior and the fruits of that will show in our lives and our relationships.

Nothing in life is easy. Our Creator never promised it would be. But, with our maturity in faith, our supportive relationships, His strength, and The Word, we can get through anything. Some adoptions may be more challenging than others, but, in the end, it's all about being obedient to what He needs us to do and ministering to each other. As the saying goes, "If God calls you to it, He'll get you through it!"

Enjoy the entire process of this and have some fun! Laugh at yourselves when times get stressful, and rest in His strong arms. As the Bible says, "Give thanks always," in all situations, in good times and bad, because it all leads back to Our Heavenly Father. And it doesn't get any better than that! May God bless you for your obedience.

POINTS TO REMEMBER

1. Successful adoptions take prayer and preparation.
2. This is a life-long relationship of some type with the birth mother.
3. The relationship is ever-changing.
4. Please make special efforts to remember the birth mother, especially in the first year.
5. Keep the BIG picture in mind: adoption is just one part of God's plan.
6. It's not about you! This is about God's plan and His timing!
7. Remember to ask these two questions when there is conflict or confusion:

*What is God's will?

*What is best for the child?

The answer for the two questions above should be identical, and if the answers conflict, then return to prayer!

8.   Know the adoption laws in your state.

9.   Find an agency and attorney knowledgeable of adoption laws.

10. Adoption must be finalized in front of a judge.

11. Indian children are governed by different tribal laws.

APPENDIX A: BIRTH PLAN FOR PATIENTS PLANNING ADOPTION

Devised by Crisis Pregnancy Outreach

Patient_____

Due Date_____

Today's Date_____

Do you want to be a confidential (No-Information) patient?

_____Yes _____No If you decide to be a No Information patient, it will be your responsibility to let your friends and family know how to contact you. Hospital policy states that as a No Information patient, the hospital cannot give out your phone number, room number, or even acknowledge that you are a patient.

I do_____ do not_____want the birth father present during delivery

I do_____ do not_____want the birth father present during the hospital stay

I do_____ do not_____want the adoptive parents present at delivery

I do_____ do not_____want the adoptive parents to stay at the hospital, during my hospital stay

I want to receive information about my baby: Yes____ No_____

I would like to hold my baby in the delivery room after he/she is born: Yes_____No_____

I would like to have my baby brought to my room during my hospital stay: Yes_____No_____ On request_____

I want to participate in caring for my baby after delivery: Yes_____ No_____Undecided_____

The names of the adoptive parents are:_____ _____

The adoptive parents may have access to the baby while he/she is in the hospital: Yes_____No_____

I would like for the adoptive parents to room-in with the baby while he/she is in the hospital: Yes_____ No_____

Who will order the baby pictures: _____ _____

Who would you like to have cut the cord, provided this is an option?

In the event of an emergency C-section, who will be going with you into the operating room? _____

___ _____

You will receive one bracelet that will allow you to go into the nursery, or have the baby in your room. Who will wear the other bracelet?

_____

If the baby is a boy, is circumcision desired?
Yes_____No_____
Decision to be made by adoptive parents_____

I would like for the baby's doctor to visit me:
Yes_____No_____

I would like a copy of the Complimentary Birth Certificate with the baby's footprints on it: Yes_____
No_____

Who will the baby be discharged to?

Agency representative_____Attorney_____

Adoptive parents_____

_____

Adoption Agency/Attorney

_____

_____

Address

_____

_____

City, State,Zip

_____

_____

All possible phone numbers (office, cell, pager)

_____

_____

Date

Used with permission by Crisis Pregnancy Outreach

APPENDIX B: ACKNOWLEDGMENT OF BIRTH FAMILY

Devised by Crisis Pregnancy Outreach

We _____

_____, acknowledge that our child _____

_____, has a birth family. By

signing this form, we promise to:

- Always speak of this family in an honoring manner
- Consider them to be a part of our extended family
- Provide them with regular letters, pictures and videos (10-15 pictures every 3 months)

- Make them feel welcome in our home, or a place that is mutually agreed upon
- Remember the birth mother and/or birth father on Holidays and other Special Days
- Give the birth mother and/or birth father our home or cell phone number or our pager number
- Treat the family with respect and affection
- Call them on a regular basis, provided they have a phone

The only behaviors that could make us suspend contact with the birth family would be:

- Their use of drugs or alcohol
- Their making any kind of threatening remarks to us, or our extended family
- Their attempt to alienate our child's relationship with us
- Their request that we not contact them

_____

_____

Signatures

Date

RESOURCES:

1. Henry T. Blackaby & Claude V. King, Experiencing God, LifeWay Press, 1990.

2. Elisabeth Kubler-Ross, M.D., On Death and Dying, Touchstone Publishers, 1969.

3. Harriet Lerner, The Dance of Anger, Harper & Row Publishing, Inc., 1985.

4. Simon & Simon, "Forgiven," Shape, January 1991.

5. Lewis B. Smedes, Ph.D., "Forgiving: The Healing Secret," Modern Maturity, December 1986-January 1987.

Made in the USA
Middletown, DE
27 December 2016